SLAVS!

Thinking About the Longstanding Problems of Virtue and Happiness

Tony Kushner

56 E 81st St., NY NY 10028–0202
212–772–8334/FAX 772–8358

SLAVS!
© Copyright 1996 by Tony Kushner

First printing: October 1996
ISBN: 0-88145-124-X

Book design: Marie Donovan
Word processing: Microsoft Word for Windows
Typographic controls: Xerox Ventura Publisher 2.0 PE
Typeface: Palatino
Printed on recycled acid-free paper and bound in the
USA.

ABOUT THE AUTHOR

Tony Kushner's plays include A BRIGHT ROOM
CALLED DAY; THE ILLUSION, freely adapted from
Corneille (published together by Broadway Play
Publishing Inc in a collection entitled PLAYS BY TONY
KUSHNER); ANGELS IN AMERICA, A Gay Fantasia
on National Themes, Part One: MILLENIUM
APPROACHES and Part Two: PERESTROIKA; and
adaptations of Goethe's STELLA, Brecht's THE GOOD
PERSON OF SETZUAN, and Ansky's THE DYBBUK
(also published by Broadway Play Publishing Inc).

His work has been produced at theaters around the
United States, including New York Theater Workshop,
the New York Shakespeare Festival, The Mark Taper
Forum, Berkeley Repertory, Steppenwolf Theater,
and Hartford Stage; on Broadway at the Walter Kerr
Theater; at the Royal National Theater in London, The
Abbey Theater in Dublin, The Deutsches Theater in
Berlin, and in over thirty countries around the world.

ANGELS IN AMERICA has been awarded the 1993
Pulitzer Prize for Drama, the 1993 and 1994 Tony
Awards for Best Play, the 1993 and 1994 Drama Desk
Awards, The 1992 Evening Standard Award, two
Olivier Award nominations, and the 1993 New York
Drama Critics Circle Award for Drama, among others.
Mr Kushner is the recipient of grants from the New

York State Council on the Arts, and the National Endowment for the Arts, a 1990 Whiting Foundation Writer's Award, and an Arts Award from the American Academy of Arts and Letters, among others. Mr Kushner was born in Manhattan and grew up in Lake Charles, Louisiana. He has a B A from Columbia University and an M F A in directing from N Y U, where he studied with Carl Weber. He lives in Manhattan.

This play is for Oskar Eustis, beloved comrade.

Acknowledgments

I'm very grateful to Jon Jory and Michael Bigelow Dixon for commissioning this play and making it possible for me to complete it.

In its final shape and for many individual moments of staging, SLAVS! and its author owe a lot to Lisa Peterson, who directed it hot-off-the-laser printer at the Actors Theater of Louisville, and in its New York incarnation.

SLAVS! was commissioned by and premiered at Actors Theater of Louisville. It subsequently was produced in New York by New York Theater Workshop.

CHARACTERS

FIRST BABUSHKA: *A snow sweep of indeterminate age.*

SECOND BABUSHKA: *Another snow sweep of indeterminate age.*

VASSILY VOROVILICH SMUKOV: *A high-ranking Politburo member, a pessimistic man in his seventies.*

SERGE ESMERELDOVICH UPGOBKIN: *A high-ranking Politburo member, an optimistic man in his eighties.*

ALEKSII ANTEDILLUVIANOVICH PRELAPSARIANOV: *A Politburo member of incalculable rank, the world's oldest living Bolshevik, considerably older than ninety.*

IPPOLITE IPPOVOLITOVICH POPOLITIPOV: *An apparatchik of some importance, a sour man in his sixties.*

YEGOR TREMENS RODENT: *An apparatchik of less importance, attached to* POPOLITIPOV; *a nervous type in his fifties.*

KATHERINA SERAFIMA GLEB: *A security guard at the Pan-Soviet Archives for the Study of Cerebro-Cephalognomical Historico-Biological Materialism (also known as PASOVACERCEPHHIBIMAT). An inebriated young woman in her twenties.*

BONFILA BEZHUKHOVNA BONCH-BRUEVICH: *A pediatric oncologist, a pleasant woman in her thirties.*

BIG BABUSHKA: *Yet another snow sweep of indeterminate age, garrulous, large, with a moustache.*

MRS SHASTLIVYI DOMIK: *An unhappy, angry woman in her forties.*

VODYA DOMIK: *A silent little girl, eight years old.*

The play takes place in Moscow, March 1985, and Talmenka, Siberia, 1992.

AUTHOR'S NOTES

For the information on the Soviet nuclear catastrophe
which is addressed in Act Three, I am indebted
primarily to a series of articles by John-Thor Dahlburg
which ran in the *Los Angeles Times*, September 2-4, 1992;
to Grigori Medvedev's *The Truth About Chernobyl*; and
to Dr Don Pizzarello of New York University Medical
Center.

In performance: When I wrote the play, I intended that
the actors should speak with very, very mild Russian
accents—standard American accents, really, lightly
perfumed with something Slavic. I now believe this to
be a mistake! In the Berkeley Rep production, Tony
Taccone, the director, and I decided to try the play with
the actors speaking in their own American accents, with
all the differences of region and class; and the results
were, unsurprisingly, more clarity and more
immediacy. And this is, after all, an American play.
The choice of accents is up to the producing company,
but be warned: no matter how much fun it is to speak
like Boris Badenov and Natasha Fatale, a possibly-fatal
distance is created by the cartoony Russian accents.
And a lot of good acting energy goes into shaping silly
sounds.

Also in performance: The FIRST and SECOND BABUSHKAs
might be played by the actresses playing DR
BONCH-BRUEVICH and MRS DOMIK. The BIG BABUSHKA
might be played by the actor playing SMUKOV.

The play's been done in a number of ways: one actor, age, and gender appropriate, per part; but also with a wonderful all-female cast; Michael Grief did it at La Jolla Playhouse with five adult actors (POPPY and RODENT are men, the other parts are played by three women) and the child. I think that a certain inventiveness in casting can be a good thing for the play.

And another thing: Status is very important. PRELAPSARIANOV is the highest-ranking Politburo member of the five; UPGOBKIN is next; then SMUKOV *(probably a military man)*; then, lower by several degrees, POPOLITIPOV; then, lowest of all, RODENT. The lesser are careful with, and polite to, the greater. POPOLITIPOV is incomparably more powerful than KATHERINA, who pays no attention to the fact. He is more powerful than, and also dangerous to, BONFILA, who is acutely aware of this. In Act Three, RODENT is now the good-will ambassador of a democratically elected federal government, the problem being that RODENT has no good will, and he both bitterly resents and desperately needs his job. In addition to the coward he has always been, he has become a closet fascist. For BONCH-BRUEVICH and MRS DOMIK, he is the first representative of real power they've seen, in years, and as such is both an opportunity and a target for their great frustration, rage and grief.

The stakes are very high. *Make sure there's an exciting EVENT transpiring on stage in every scene! Stakes! Goals! Action! Too many times the characters seem to be chatting while waiting for a bus to arrive.*

The first act is treacherous!
The first act is delicate. It's a big mistake to strain towards big laughs in the first few scenes. This is not a farce, not a knockabout comedy! When the play is being performed you have to remember that the audience is

being ushered instantly into an unfamiliar world—the history; the theoretical, rhetorical, poetic speech; the political, moral, romantic passion are all unfamiliar— and the audience must be relaxed in order to listen to what the characters are saying. And the most important thing is that the ideas are clear, that the language sings. The action of much of the first act is *to think*—about the longstanding problems of virtue and happiness— a lively, active, vigorous, passionate thinking, not introspective brooding, but *thinking hard, discussing*.

I suggest a flexibly hieratic staging of the scene in Act One, according to which the actors are grouped in arrangements that help make the argument clear, that reveal the position each character represents on the political spectrum—for instance, that the real dialectic here is between UPGOBKIN (true progress) and POPOLITIPOV (true reaction), with SMUKOV and RODENT trying to keep up, and PRELAPSARIANOV representing a third term, a synthesis.

These all are people who speak their thoughts, rather than people who think and then speak. There is no need for pausing to arrive at an idea or an articulation— the rhetorical grandeur is second nature for them, expressive of great Slavic passion. However, the lack of struggle to find words does not mean that the specific words they choose are unimportant to them—language is everything. As is politics, the air they breathe; as is love.

If it seems desirable to help the audience know where it is (I recommend it), taped voice-over introductions can be played before the following scenes:

Before Act One, Scene One

Voice on tape: *(Russian accent, of course)* An anteroom outside the Chamber of Deputies, the Kremlin. Moscow, March 1985.

Before Act One, Scene Two

(On tape the babble of hundreds of voices arguing passionately. The sound of a gavel pounding the rostrum in an immense hall. The crowd gets quieter but not silent. A voice exclaims:)

Voice on tape: Comrades! Comrades! Aleksii Antedilluvianovich Prelapsarianov! *(Then in a whisper:)* The world's oldest living Bolshevik....

Before Act Two, Scene One

Voice on tape: The guards' chamber of the Pan-Soviet Archives for the Study of Cerebro-Cephalognomical Historico-Biological Materialism, also known as PASOVACERCEPHHIBIMAT. Moscow, March 1985.

(Note: PASOVACERCEPHHIBIMAT is pronounced "passovah-sayr-seff-HIB-i-mat.")

Before Act Three, Scene One

Voice on tape: A medical facility. Talmenka, Siberia, 1992.

PROLOGUE

(Two BABUSHKAS, *dressed in knee-length cheap winter coats, their legs encased in thick white support hose, their feet shod in rubber galoshes, their heads of course wrapped in floral- or geometric-print scarves tied under the chin, are sweeping snow from the entrance steps of the Hall of the Soviets, the Kremlin, March 1985. As they sweep, the snow falls. They talk:)*

FIRST BABUSHKA

However reluctant one may be to grant it, history and the experience of this century presses upon us the inescapable conclusion that there is a direct continuum from Dictatorship of the Proletariat and the embrace of violence as a means of effecting change that one finds in later Marx and Engels, to dictatorship plain and simple—you missed a spot—and state terror.

SECOND BABUSHKA

True enough. But Marx's defense of revolutionary violence must be set in its proper context, namely: the nineteenth-century evolutionary-socialist error-of-belief in the Inevitability of Gradualism, which sought not so much to transform society into something new....

FIRST BABUSHKA

...But rather to create merely an "improved" version of the society one sought to change.

SECOND BABUSHKA
Exactly.

FIRST BABUSHKA
But is it not a false antinomy to predicate as the
only alternative to Reformism or Gradualism a
vanguard-driven....

*(Two Politburo members, VASSILY VOROVILICH SMUKOV
and SERGE ESMERELDOVICH UPGOBKIN, very impressive
in greatcoats and big fur hats, enter.)*

SECOND BABUSHKA
(Seeing them) Shhhh! Shhhhhh!

(The BABUSHKAS clam up tight. They sweep.)

SMUKOV
Morning, Grandma.

*(The BABUSHKAS suddenly become sweet, toothless old
ladies, smiling, head-bobbing, forelock-tugging mumblers.)*

FIRST BABUSHKA
Good morning, Sirs!

SECOND BABUSHKA
How-de-doo! Mind the ice, don't slip!

(UPGOBKIN and SMUKOV start up the steps.)

FIRST BABUSHKA
Big doings today, Sirs...

SMUKOV
Oh, the usual Mischief...

UPGOBKIN
(Watching them sweep) Heavy snows for March.
Your labor, I fear, is Sisyphean!

SECOND BABUSHKA

And what's more, Sir, it's completely pointless!
We sweep, it falls, we sweep some more, it falls
some more...

FIRST BABUSHKA

It's hopeless, hopeless!

(The two BABUSHKAS *laugh and laugh.)*

SMUKOV

That's the spirit, Grandma! Sweep! Sweep!

(The BABUSHKAS *sweep; they are all laughing.* SMUKOV
and UPGOBKIN *take each other's arm, climb the stairs, and
disappear into the Hall. The* BABUSHKAS *instantly stop
laughing.)*

FIRST BABUSHKA

So where was I?

SECOND BABUSHKA

...a vanguard-driven...

FIRST BABUSHKA

Yes! A vanguard-driven revolution as the only
alternative to Reaction. For the People make their
own history.

SECOND BABUSHKA

Limits are set by the conditions of their social
development.

FIRST BABUSHKA

But those conditions are themselves affected by the
state of their economic relations. *(She stops sweeping.)*
Sweeping snow. In Moscow. It is Sisyphean.

SECOND BABUSHKA

(A shrug) Nevertheless. Sweep, "Grandma."

FIRST BABUSHKA

Grandma yourself. *(Sweeping again)* Big doings today...

SECOND BABUSHKA

Big.

ACT ONE

Scene One

(In an anteroom outside the Politburo Chamber in the Hall of the Soviets in the Kremlin, March 1985. SMUKOV and UPGOBKIN, in suits now, are sitting and talking. A samovar stands nearby, brewing tea.)

SMUKOV

People are not capable of change. They used to be, maybe, but not anymore. In the old days you could ask anything of the people and they'd do it: Live without bread, without heat in the winter, take a torch to their own houses—as long as they believed they were building socialism there was no limit to how much they could adapt, transform. Moldable clay in the hands of history.

UPGOBKIN

And you feel it's different now?

SMUKOV

Well, you see. We are all grown less pliable, unsure of our footing, unsure of the way, brittle bones and cataracts.... How are your cataracts, by the way, Serge Esmereldovich?

UPGOBKIN

(Shrugs) Old eyes get tough, cloudy. This one *(Points to one eye)* is not really an eye anymore, it's a bottle cork,

it's a walnut. This one *(Points to the other eye)* lets in
milky light. I live in a world of milk-white ghosts now,
luminous beings, washed clean of detail. And I hear
better, Vashka: in every voice, a million voices
whispering. *(Imitates whispering; it sounds like the sea.)*
Sssssshhhhh, shhssshhh... More tea?

SMUKOV

No; I'll have to get up to pee in the middle of Aleksii's
speech.

UPGOBKIN

Whereas I intend to drink two more cups, so the
pressure on my bladder will keep me awake.

SMUKOV

At least in the bad old days you could sleep through the
speeches and not worry that you'd miss a thing. Now
the speeches are longer and you have to stay awake to
boo. It's miserable, democracy. Grishin or Gorbachev,
Gorbachev or Grishin. I vote not to vote! I am a true
apostle of the old scientific creed: Geriatrical
Materialism. Our motto: Stagnation is our only hope.
Our sacred text: Silence. Not this interminable debate,
blah blah blah, my side, your side—really, this is
logorrhea, not revolution.

UPGOBKIN

Patience.
   There are no shortcuts to the new era. The terrain
is vast. Aeons to traverse, everything is implicated,
everything encompassed, the world, the universe....
   Today this anteroom is the anteroom to History,
Vashka! Beyond those doors, inside that chamber,
History is aborning! Inhale its perfumes! A harsh and
unnaturally protracted winter is losing its teeth. A great
pressure has built up to this, Vashka, a great public
desperation. There is no choice. You'll see that people

can change, and change radically. From crown to toe,
every cell formed anew. We set the process in motion
with our words.

SMUKOV

People, I think, would rather die than change.

UPGOBKIN

Do you really think so?
I believe precisely the opposite.
We would rather change than die.
We have been ordered into motion by History herself,
Vashka. When the sun comes out, the sky cracks open,
the silent flowers twist and sway...

Scene Two

(ALEKSII ANTEDILLUVIANOVICH PRELAPSARIANOV
*the world's oldest Bolshevik, speaking in the Chamber of
Deputies. He is unimaginably old and totally blind. His voice
is thin and high, but he speaks with great passion.)*

PRELAPSARIANOV

And Theory? Theory? How are we to proceed without
Theory? Is it enough to reject the past, is it wise to move
forward in this blind fashion, without the Cold Brilliant
Light of Theory to guide the way? What have these
reformers to offer in the way of Theory? What beautiful
system of thought have they to present to the world,
to the befuddling, contrary tumult of life, to this mad
swirling planetary disorganization, to the Inevident
Welter of fact, event, phenomenon, calamity? Do they
have, as we did, a beautiful Theory, as bold, as Grand,
as comprehensive a construct...? You can't imagine,
when we first read the Classic Texts, when in the
dark-vexed night of our ignorance and terror the
seed-words sprouted and shoved incomprehension

aside, when the incredible bloody vegetable struggled
up and through into Red Blooming, gave us Praxis,
True Praxis, True Theory married to Actual Life....
You who live in this Sour Little Age cannot imagine
the sheer grandeur of the prospect we gazed upon:
Like standing atop the highest peak in the mighty
Caucasus, and viewing in one all-knowing glance the
mountainous, granite order of creation. We were One
with the Sidereal Pulse then, in the blood in our heads
we heard the tick of the Infinite. You cannot imagine it.
I weep for you.

And what have you to offer now, children of this
Theory? What have you to offer in its place? Market
Incentives? Watered-down Bukharinite stopgap
makeshift Capitalism? NEPmen! Pygmy children
of a gigantic race!

Change? Yes, we must must change, only show me
the Theory, and I will be at the barricades, show me the
book of the next Beautiful Theory, and I promise you
these blind eyes will see again, just to read it, to devour
that text. Show me the words that will reorder the
world, or else keep silent.

The snake sheds its skin only when a new skin is
ready; if he gives up the only membrane he has before
he can replace it, naked he will be in the world, prey
to the forces of chaos: without his skin he will be
dismantled, lose coherence, and die. Have you, my
little serpents, a new skin?

Then we dare not, we cannot move ahead.

Scene Three

(*Outside the Chamber of Deputies again, the Kremlin.*
IPPOLITE IPPOVOLITOVICH POPOLITIPOV *and* YEGOR
TREMENS RODENT, *two middle-aged deputies, are talking.*
POPOLITIPOV *is in a rage over the debate in the adjoining*

chamber. RODENT *is freaked out.* RODENT *is* POPOLITIPOV's
protégé, and is profoundly deferential.)

POPOLITIPOV

The heart is not progressive. The heart is conservative,
no matter what the mind may be. Why don't they get
that? The mind may make its leaps ahead; the heart will
refuse to budge, shatter at the prospect. Yearn to go
back to what it loves. That's the function of the organ,
that's what it's there for: to fall in love. And love is
profoundly reactionary, you fall in love and that instant
is fixed, love is always fixed on the past.

RODENT

Oh true. Oh I am all terror these days. Sleep with the
light on. No idea of what: just terror. Popolitipov, look!
I'm shaking!

POPOLITIPOV

Now debate that, reformers! The conservative, fractable
human heart!

*(*UPGOBKIN, *leading* PRELAPSARIANOV *to a comfy chair.)*

RODENT

(To POPOLITIPOV*)* Sssshhhh.

*(*POPOLITIPOV *and* RODENT *move a discreet distance away
from the two old Bolsheviks.)*

PRELAPSARIANOV

(As UPGOBKIN *helps him to his chair)* Stop hovering,
Serge Esmereldovich, you're practically buggering me!

UPGOBKIN

I have to stand this close, otherwise I don't see...

PRELAPSARIANOV

Nothing to see! I'm fine! And your breath is terrible. Please, you give me the fidgets. It's just a vein, just a weak vein in my head.

UPGOBKIN

I'll get some tea for you.... (*Looking about*) If I can find the samovar.

RODENT

There, comrade Upgobkin, it's over there....

PRELAPSARIANOV

I'm the blind one! You just have cataracts! I'm blind!

POPOLITIPOV

Is Comrade Minister Prelapsarianov not feeling well?

PRELAPSARIANOV

HOURS! HOURS OF TALK! What do they think they have to say! Such pretentiousness, they fart and they whinny and I HAVE AN ANEURYSM! (*He has gotten overexcited.*) Oh, oh, oh...

UPGOBKIN

Some hot tea... (*He pours in a stiff shot of vodka from a hip flask.*)

POPOLITIPOV

(*Quietly, to* RODENT) For decades a mostly respectable torpor. Now: Expect madness.

RODENT

(*Also quiet*) In Omsk thousands saw a radiant orb in the sky, larger than the moon. Sea monsters were seen swimming in some Kazakhstan lake. Strange space creatures reported landed in Gorki...

POPOLITIPOV
With three eyes. And they marched about the square.

RODENT
Six eyes. Tiny tiny head, big big body, six eyes.

POPOLITIPOV
I really think it was only three.

RODENT
Two rows of three each, which makes six.

POPOLITIPOV
Aha.

UPGOBKIN
(Offering the teacup to PRELAPSARIANOV*)* Can you
swallow it?

PRELAPSARIANOV
My head, my head, inside my brain, there's an itch, a
little worm.... Sssshhhh. Sssshhhh... *(He cradles his head.)*

RODENT
The theory is that radioactivity escaped from the
explosion at the plutonium plant at Mayak is calling to
them, the creatures, from across space, and they come
perhaps with food and magic farm equipment, or
personal computers, or with death rays to kill us all,
and in Novy Sibirsk, people whose grandparents were
merely babies when the Czar was killed are rumored to
have used black arts to resurrect.... Rasputin. Rasputin.

POPOLITIPOV
This cannot be what Lenin intended.

RODENT

Fantasy is the spiritual genius of Slavic peoples.
 And icons weep blood again. As if seventy years
of socialism had never happened at all.

PRELAPSARIANOV

(Sitting suddenly bolt upright) Wait. Wait. OH! OH!

UPGOBKIN

Aleksii? Aleksii!

RODENT

Is Comrade Minister all right, is...

(PRELAPSARIANOV *stands, staring ahead, dropping the
teacup.*)

POPOLITIPOV

Serge Esmereldovich, is he...?

PRELAPSARIANOV

I see it now! Now I see! For ninety years I have
wondered and wondered and wondered WHY is the
Good Cause always defeated by the Bad, WHY Injustice
and never Justice anywhere, WHY does Evil always
always triumph and Good cast down in the gutter to
be shat upon, WHY THIS HORROR AND WHY THIS
HEARTACHE and NOW I GET IT! Because God...is a
Menshevik! Because God...is a Petty-Bourgeois! Because
God is a Reactionary, and Progressive People are THE
POLITICAL ENEMIES OF GOD! He HATES US! Now!
Now AT LAST I SEE— *(He collapses and dies.)*

UPGOBKIN

Aleksii? Aleksii!?

RODENT

Oh my God...

UPGOBKIN

Oh help, oh help, oh somebody, somebody,
Aleksii Antedilluvianovich Prelapsarianov is dead!

Scene Four

(SMUKOV *enters.*)

SMUKOV

Did I hear...? Oh my. A dead body.

UPGOBKIN

Aleksii Antedilluvianovich Prelapsarianov is dead.

SMUKOV

Oh dear, he spoke too long. So many words, we were
afraid this might happen.

POPOLITIPOV

The strain on the heart.

RODENT

No, it was his brain. A vessel popped upstairs. His face
is royal purple.

POPOLITIPOV

But popped because: The grieving heart avenged itself
on the forward-moving mind. The heart drowned the
brain in blood. So that the whole animal could rest, safe
from the future, secure in the past. As I was saying, the
mind may....

RODENT

Someone ought to call Security, we can't leave him
lying....

UPGOBKIN

His heart had little reason to murder his mind, Ippolite Ippopolitovich, Aleksii's mind was hardly moving in a forward direction.

SMUKOV

I thought in the main his arguments were sound. As I understood it....

POPOLITIPOV

The brain inhabits the body like a virus inhabits a cell. It takes control of the nucleus and selfishly mismanages the entirety till disaster results. It does not do to think too much! You reformers, you vanguard, you taskmaster brain....

RODENT

Oh you are making too much of this, Poppy, Comrade Minister Prelapsarianov was ninety-five years old. No wonder, it was past his time.

POPOLITIPOV

Illness is a metaphor, Yegor; the human body, the body politic, the human soul, the soul of the state. Dynamic and immobile all at once, lava and granite, the head and the heart. It's all tension and tearing, and which will win? An infarction (Clutches his heart) or a stroke? (Clutches his head)

SMUKOV

I don't know what you're talking about, Popolitipov, but one thing is clear: We should not move until we know where we're going. They should chisel that on poor Aleksii's tombstone, that was his best bit. Wait patiently till the way is clear.

UPGOBKIN

And imagination? That faculty? Which Angels are said
to lack, but people possess? Dialectics can only lead us
so far, to the edge of what is known. But after that...?
We see so poorly, almost blind. We who....

RODENT

Careful, Serge Esmereldovich, if you're going to make
a speech, look at what happened to poor Comrade
Minister, and you're almost as old as he is...was.

UPGOBKIN

Then let me follow him into oblivion. Let me make that
leap. Because you can only creep so far, and then you
must leap, Rodent, you must use your own legs and
your own will, or life itself will simply toss you in the
air, but willing or resisting, I promise you all, you will
leap! Does the heart plot to kill the mind, does it shatter
that not-sprouted seed, the brain, before the New
Blooms blossom? Then let the heart beware, for my
brain will dream the New, I will make that leap, and
let the strain be too much, let the strain explode my
recalcitrant heart, let my heart burst like a bomb while
my sparks leap their synapses! We must dream the
New! And by Caution we never can! By Leaping!
*(He begins to leap in the air, over and over, going higher
and higher.)*

POPOLITIPOV

Stop it, Serge Esmereldovich Upgobkin, you'll...

UPGOBKIN

(As he leaps, to POPOLITIPOV*)* Leap, you unregenerate
Stalinist! Leap, you bursitic Brezhnevite! Leap, leap,
Procrustean, legless Legachevite, leap!
   So what if they dissolve the entire Union, so what if
the Balkans are all re-Balkanized, so what if the Ukraine
won't sell us their wheat, and Georgia secedes, and

Germany reunites, and all our reforms go only to
squelch real revolution!

SMUKOV

Oh, well, now that would really be terrible, we...

UPGOBKIN

(Still leaping, continuing over the above, to SMUKOV*)*
LEAP! HIGH! See if you can see it! The NEW! The
UNIMAGINED! The THAT-FOR-WHICH-OUR-
DREAMS-ARE-ACHING! For what is hope but
desiring forwards!? *(To* RODENT*)* Are you a man, or are
you a mollusc? Will you never dare? Will you be dead
forever?

RODENT

NO!

UPGOBKIN

Then LEAP!

*(*UPGOBKIN *and* RODENT *leap and leap.)*

SMUKOV

Serge, Serge, please don't overexert yourself, what has
gotten into you?

UPGOBKIN

The NEW! The NEW! The NEW!

POPOLITIPOV

(Over the above) Yegor Tremens Rodent, stop that at
once!

*(*POPOLITIPOV *stops* RODENT, *pulls him down to earth.)*

POPOLITIPOV

Control yourself, dammit.

SMUKOV

Look at him! Serge...

(UPGOBKIN *is leaping higher and higher. His face is upturned, he is no longer with his comrades, he is beatific, he is smiling enormously. From above there is a violently brief burst of radiance, and the instant it falls on* UPGOBKIN *he collapses and dies. And the light is gone.)*

RODENT

Now I am calling Security. And no more metaphors, anyone, please.

Two bodies, two bodies, what a scandal this will make.

POPOLITIPOV

Was it his heart, or was it his head?

RODENT

Heart.

SMUKOV

Still smiling. That smile. What on Earth do you suppose he saw?

(They look up, wondering.)

ACT TWO

Scene One

(*In the small, dank, dark, dismal room that serves as the guards' chamber of the Pan-Soviet Archives for the Study of Cerebro-Cephalognomical Historico-Biological Materialism [also known as PASOVACERCEPHHIBIMAT, pronounced "passovah-sayr-seff-HIB-i-mat"]. The night following the afternoon of Act One. A table for a desk, an old swivel chair missing a wheel, and a security-system video monitor surveilling an adjoining room in which big glass jars sit in neat rows on shelves. In the jars float human brains. [We see this room only on the video screen.] In the guardroom, KATHERINA SERAFIMA GLEB, a young woman in her twenties who is wearing the uniform of a security guard, is sitting, staring into space. An old samovar, much less impressive than the samovar in Act One, stands on the table, brewing tea. POPOLITIPOV, wearing a voluminous greatcoat and a big fur hat, covered in snow, bursts in, carrying an ancient, battered guitar case.*)

POPOLITIPOV

You.

KATHERINA

What?

POPOLITIPOV

Have replaced myself in me.

KATHERINA

What?

POPOLITIPOV

The soul in me that on Judgment Day looked to ascend to bright Heaven has been smitten, obliterated, replaced in me by you.

KATHERINA

Too creepy.

POPOLITIPOV

I am not merely yours, Katherina, I am you, I have become you.

KATHERINA

I said, too creepy.

POPOLITIPOV

I would like to run my tongue against the salty soft shag covering your upper lip.

KATHERINA

Too personal.

POPOLITIPOV

I want to fuck you.

KATHERINA

Don't try anything, Poppy, I'm warning you.

POPOLITIPOV

Can I sing you a song?

KATHERINA

Your voice is repulsive. No. Do you have cigarettes?

POPOLITIPOV

No. In me there is a yearning, and it complains to me of
wanting you, it strains against my skin towards you, it
is like the wet lapping of the tide, the pull of the moon
on the ocean, like the rise of sap through frozen wood
when winter is shattered by the brunt thrust of spring.

KATHERINA

Too romantic.

POPOLITIPOV

Like the hydraulic rush of the river through the dam,
the whine of turbines, voltage coursing across a
continent of wire.

KATHERINA

Too technological.

POPOLITIPOV

Like the inchoate voluptuous seething of the masses as
they surge towards revolutionary consciousness.

KATHERINA

(Overlapping on "surge") Too political. Too corny.

POPOLITIPOV

When I was a child...

KATHERINA

Too psychological.

POPOLITIPOV

(Screams, then:) Give yourself to me, I beg you,
Katherina Serafima, or I will blow my brains out,
I will lie down in a snowbank or under a train or....

KATHERINA

You were supposed to bring cigarettes, Poppy.

POPOLITIPOV

I burn my flesh with cigarettes, dreaming of you,
I scrape my knuckles along roughcast walls—look,
bloody scabs—I deliberately lace my shoes too tight,
and cinch my belt till my intestines squirm under
pressure, in pain, I refuse myself sleep, dreaming of
you, I've slept maybe six, maybe seven hours this
whole month, sleep-deprived, trussed and hobbled,
and why? I mean, are you clever? No. Are you kind?
Most certainly not. And yet there is in all your
attributes considered and parts taken together a
summational, additive kind of perfection: I love you.

KATHERINA

You're old.

POPOLITIPOV

I love you.

KATHERINA

I hate you.

POPOLITIPOV

(Shouting) I LOVE YOU!

KATHERINA

I'm a lesbian.

POPOLITIPOV

Pervert.

KATHERINA

Asshole.

POPOLITIPOV

Abomination!

KATHERINA

Exploiter!

POPOLITIPOV

Wanton! Abuser!

KATHERINA

Harasser! Torturer! Apparatchik!

(He lunges for her. She dodges easily. He falls heavily.
She steps on his neck.)

KATHERINA

I warned you.

POPOLITIPOV

Get off.

KATHERINA

Cigarettes.

(He hands them to her. She releases him.)

KATHERINA

I'm tired of this, Poppy, I'm going to find an easier way
to get a decent smoke. I really am a lesbian, you know.
I have a new girlfriend. I'll never have sex with you,
I don't want to touch you, and frankly, Poppy, it's not
fair you should make me go through this mortifying
business over and over and over again, night after night
after night; know what? You're a pig.

POPOLITIPOV

I cannot help myself. *(He begins to remove an ancient*
guitar from the guitar case.)

KATHERINA

Just because you got me a soft job. A soft, boring job.
Which I hate. This place is creepy. Know what? At
night I hear them slithering.

POPOLITIPOV

Who?

KATHERINA

The brains. They rub their spongy rivules and volutes
against the smooth glass sides of their jars. Sometimes
they bubble. As if breathing.

POPOLITIPOV

The brains are dead brains, Katherina.

KATHERINA

Then why don't they throw them out?

POPOLITIPOV

They study them. The great minds of the Party.
Political minds. Scientific minds. Even an artist or two.

KATHERINA

In my opinion they should throw them out. Most of
the older ones are falling apart. No one could make a
proper study of them. Sometimes when I get bored,
I grab the jars and shake them up. The brain cells of
Vyshinsky. The brain cells of Iron Feliks Dzerzhinsky.
Whirl like snowflakes in a crystal snowball.

POPOLITIPOV

Become my mistress or I will report you.

KATHERINA

When you die, Poppy, will they put your brain in a jar?

(POPOLITIPOV *begins to play softly, serenading her.*)

KATHERINA

(*Listens to the music a beat, then:*) Some nights I pretend
that I am not simply night watchman but I lead
midnight tours through here for insomniac Muscovites
whose anxieties or guilty consciences keep them awake.
This is my speech: (*To the audience*) Welcome to
PASOVACERCEPHHIBIMAT, also known as The
Pan-Soviet Archives for the Study of

Cerebro-Cephalognomical Historico-Biological
Materialism. Here the Party has stored the brains of its
bygone leaders, an unbroken line of brains stretching
back to Red October. Beginning of course with Lenin,
most people think his brain is still in his body in the
crypt, but it's not, it's here, it is MASSIVE, 1,340 grams
of solid brain-flesh, the heaviest brain ever extracted,
it's a wonder the poor man could hold his head up his
brain was so grotesquely HUGE. Ranked beside it are
many other famous brains, all floating in some sort of
sudsy lime-green mummifying juice, all the famous
Bolshevik brains except for those which got flushed in
the notorious dead-brain Purges of 1937. Stalin's brain
is here; Brezhnev's, which is dingy-yellow like an old
tooth; Andropov's, and now I suppose Chernenko's; he
died last week but his brain's not here yet: Maybe they
couldn't find it. (*She goes to* POPOLITIPOV *and tousle-pulls
his hair. Teasingly, torturing him:*) Let's talk politics.

POPOLITIPOV

(*Strumming*) I don't want to talk politics with you,
my Katushka, I want to pluck my guitar for you,
pick pick pick I pick my heart to pieces.

KATHERINA

Gorbachev will replace Chernenko. Right? Come on,
Poppy. Tell me! Gorbachev will be our honored leader
next? His wife is a Jewess.

POPOLITIPOV

(*Continuing to strum*) No she...

KATHERINA

That's what they say: Jewess.

(POPOLITIPOV *continues to play under this.*)

KATHERINA

I'm not an anti-Semite, I have nothing to do with Jews,
but that's what they say.
  Tea?

(POPOLITIPOV *nods his head "yes," still playing.*
KATHERINA *goes to the samovar, lifts the lid, reaches within
and withdraws an alarmingly large bottle of vodka. She takes
a huge swallow and hands it to* POPOLITIPOV, *who does the
same. While he drinks, she hums his tune, and then he starts
playing again. Throughout all this the music never stops.*)

POPOLITIPOV

Gorbachev isn't a Jew. Nor is Raisa Maxsimovna.
She just likes to dress fancy. A strange lust for the sort
of pleasures one associates with adolescence seems to
have overtaken everyone: panic, mania, nausea, rage.
The pleasures of adulthood are forsaken.

KATHERINA

What are the pleasures of adulthood?

POPOLITIPOV

Heartbreak. Agony deep as bone marrow.
Quiet, nuanced despair.

(*He looks at her. She drinks vodka. He drinks vodka.
He plays again.*)

KATHERINA

Gorbachev will come, trailing free-market anarchy in
his wake! Burger King! Pizza Hut! The International
Monetary Fund! Billions in aid will flow! Solzhenitsyn
will come back from Vermont to thrash and purify us!
Kentucky Fried Chicken franchises! Toxic waste!
Everything will change then, because Gorbachev is
crafty and sly in the manner of Jews. He'll defeat the
deadbeat nomenklatura, every last one, including you,
Poppy, and then there will be no more politics, we will

become like Americans, I will be in a heavy-metal band!
There will be surprises: most of them unpleasant, but at
least unanticipated, and the Great Grey Age of
Boredom will finally lift.

(She takes a swig of vodka; he takes a swig of vodka.)

POPOLITIPOV
To the Great Age of Boredom.

KATHERINA
I am inexpressibly, immeasurably sad. Sad sad.

POPOLITIPOV
Because you are a Slav. Sorrow is the spiritual genius of
Slavic peoples.

KATHERINA
Bullshit. I don't believe in national identities.
Reactionary! I am an anarchist.

POPOLITIPOV
You are a nihilist.

KATHERINA
I am an internationalist. *(Swig of vodka)* Like Trotsky!
(Swig of vodka) The Jew!

(Pause. He looks at her.)

POPOLITIPOV
When I was a child, I was an ugly child, a graceless
child, and did not believe I would be loved and was
in fact not loved by anyone.

KATHERINA
Poor Poppy. Poor Poppy the Slav.

POPOLITIPOV

My mother dead in the Great Patriotic War, in the
snow, German bullet through her spine, her belly,
but I was already a young man by then so it can't have
been then that I lost her love, but earlier, earlier, a point
towards which my memories refuse to travel—I cannot
blame them. My father was a bastard, the Germans got
him, too.

KATHERINA

(Swigging vodka) Poppy the orphan.

POPOLITIPOV

The Party adopted me. The Party was not Love, but
Necessity; it rebuilt the ruined world. Through the
Party I came to love.

KATHERINA

Love.

(Vodka. Sorrow.)

POPOLITIPOV

The Party dispenses miracles. The Party drove away
the Czar, immortalized Lenin, withstood France and
Britain and the United States, made Communism in one
country, electrified Russia, milled steel, built railways,
abolished distance, defeated Germany, suspended time,
became Eternal, dispersed the body of each and every
member, molecule by molecule, across an inconceivably
vast starry matrix encompassing the infinite: so that,
within the Party, everything is; so that everything
human—even Marx—was shown as limited and the
Party, illimitable; and through the illimitable Party the
human is exalted, becomes Divine, occupant of a great
chiming spaciousness that is not distance but time, time
which never moves nor passes, light which does not
travel and yet is light: And love, pure love, even in a

degraded, corrupt and loveless world, love can finally
be born.

(Little pause, more vodka)

POPOLITIPOV
Do you understand what I am saying to you, Katushka?

KATHERINA
(Softly; deeply moved) Not a word.

POPOLITIPOV
(Very tenderly) That night, that night, when I saw you
that night, I was walking in the Arbat, you had fallen
in the snow, sleeping in the gutter, dirty, drunk,
rude, radiant: I was overwhelmed with lust, and then
followed love. Love. Love. Love. Love. *(They are very
close; he has almost won.)* Even in a corrupt and loveless
world, love can be born.

*(KATHERINA leaps to her feet and screams, a long, loud,
howl of joy. She rushes across the room at DR BONFILA
BEZHUKHOVNA BONCH-BRUEVICH, who is just entering
the room, carrying a wrapped parcel, wearing hat and coat,
covered in snow. KATHERINA kisses BONFILA passionately.)*

POPOLITIPOV
(Aghast!) Good GOD!

BONFILA
(Seeing POPOLITIPOV) Oh my GOD.

KATHERINA
GOD I'm happy! *(To POPOLITIPOV)* Hello, Poppy!

BONFILA
(Horror-stricken, bowing her head slightly) Comrade
Commissar, I...

KATHERINA
See? Lesbians! This is my girlfriend, Doctor Bonf...

BONFILA
(Cutting her off) I'm interrupting.

(BONFILA turns to leave; KATHERINA grabs her arm.)

KATHERINA
No, Poppy was interrupting, Poppy is always
interrupting, but now he's going. Aren't you, Poppy?
(Screaming with rage) GO, POPPY!!!

BONFILA
(To KATHARINA) You're drunk.

KATHERINA
No I'm not.

BONFILA
Yes you are!

KATHERINA
You're mad at me.
(To POPOLITIPOV) See what you've done.
I need a drink.
(To POPOLITIPOV) See, my sadness is gone, I must not
be a true Slav after all. I'm happy you can see her, now
maybe you will know that I cannot love you: ever, ever.
And she is a physician, she cures people, not an
ineffectual aged paperpushing-timeserver-apparatchik-
with-a-dacha like you who only bleeds the people dry.

(Awkward pause)

BONFILA
Did I interrupt... *(Pointing to the guitar that* POPOLITIPOV
clutches) Comrade Commissar was playing the...

POPOLITIPOV

(Putting the guitar away; very, very darkly) Not anymore.
Doctor...?

KATHERINA

Bonch-Bruevich!

BONFILA

(Simultaneously) Comrade Commissar, I...
(To KATHERINA, *hearing that she has said her name)*
Shut up.
I'll go.
I'll go.
Somebody should go.
This is mortifying.

POPOLITIPOV

Is it?
(Pleasant) Things change. Some things. We are all
liberals.
(Homicidally angry, to KATHERINA*)* Horseleech!
Viper's spawn!
(Pleasant again) You are a doctor. Of...?
(Military command) Do you have a specialty.

BONFILA

Pediatric oncology.

KATHERINA

(Sad) Kids with cancer.

POPOLITIPOV

Moscow?

BONFILA

I... Yes.

POPOLITIPOV
(*Trying to keep it together but coming unglued*) That's
convenient for both of you. You are lucky. Moscow is
an agreeable posting, for cosmopolitans such as you
and I. Many doctors have to report to places more
remote, arctic outposts.... (*Little pause; becoming suddenly
profoundly sad and weary*) Doctor, may I ask you a
health-related question?

BONFILA
Certainly.

POPOLITIPOV
(*In confidence, in earnest*) If a man were to shoot himself,
against which of the various customary vulnerable
points of the body would you advise he position the
barrel of his gun?

BONFILA
I...

POPOLITIPOV
Temple? Soft palate? Heart?

KATHERINA
I have a friend who died by shooting himself in the
armpit. The bullet went through his shoulder and into
his nose.

(KATHERINA *bursts into gales of drunken laughter. A beat.*
BONFILA *and* POPOLITIPOV *stare at* KATHERINA.)

BONFILA
(*Softly, deferentially*) I would advise him not to shoot
himself, Comrade Commissar. I would advise him to
live.

POPOLITIPOV
Say his life had become unbearable.

BONFILA

Life is almost never literally unbearable. We choose whether or not we bear up. We choose.

POPOLITIPOV

Circumstances may dictate otherwise. History.

BONFILA

People make their own history.

POPOLITIPOV

Limits are set by the conditions of their social development.

KATHERINA

(By rote, a thing she learned in school) Those conditions are themselves affected by the state of their economic relations.

(Pause. The others look at KATHERINA.*)*

KATHERINA

Which in turn are related to a particular stage of the mode of production. *(She sits heavily, slumps over, falls asleep.)*

POPOLITIPOV

(Crossing to the sleeping KATHERINA. *He looks at her, then:)* Her head is stuffed full of pottery shards, rags, ash, and wind. She is the Revolution's Great-granddaughter. She is...a barbarian.

BONFILA

She's immature. And can't drink. And I think she doesn't like you very much.

POPOLITIPOV

I must be going.

KATHERINA
(Still slumped over, drowsy) Try the armpit, Poppy.

POPOLITIPOV
(A beat; then, bracing himself for the mortal blow) If I shoot
myself, Katherina, will you miss me?

KATHERINA
(Looking up) Maybe. For a day or two. Maybe.
The cigarettes, definitely.
Not really. No.
Oh Poppy, I'm sorry, but you're a pig, you know,
and I would like to be kind, but I can't. *(She sleeps.)*

POPOLITIPOV
We have not made kind people. *(To* BONFILA, *not
without menace)* We have not made a world that makes
people kind. *(He leaves.)*

BONFILA
Is he really going to shoot himself?

*(*KATHERINA *snores, loudly.)*

Scene Two

(The guardroom. Several hours later. KATHERINA *and*
BONFILA *sit at the table, both drunk,* KATHERINA *more
drunk. The parcel, still wrapped, is on the table between
them. Also on the table is a now nearly empty bottle of vodka.)*

BONFILA
My great-grandfather was Vladimir Dimitrievich
Bonch-Bruevich. Do you know who that is?

*(*KATHERINA *shakes her head "no.")*

BONFILA

First Secretary of the Sovnarkom. The Council of
People's Commissars. 1918. A founder of the Party.

KATHERINA

Never heard of him.

BONFILA

It's your history.

KATHERINA

I have no history. What's in the package?

BONFILA

My great-grandfather is the man who embalmed Lenin.
He selected the design for the tomb.

KATHERINA

You're angry with me because I'm drunk.

BONFILA

Not as angry as I was when I was sober.

KATHERINA

Promise we'll be lovers forever.

BONFILA

No.

KATHERINA

Promise we'll be lovers 'till I'm sober.

BONFILA

Yes.

KATHERINA

If you leave me I'll kill you.

BONFILA

Oh bullshit.

KATHERINA

Is Poppy dead yet, do you think? You've been my lover
for more than a month, and look, you still visit me late
at night, you bring me mysterious packages....

BONFILA

Three weeks, it's only been... It's still new to me,
all this....

KATHERINA

You won't leave me, will you?

BONFILA

I love you.

KATHERINA

That's not what I asked. Everyone loves me, but I'm
unbearable.
I need someone who will...stay, or....
I'm sad again.

BONFILA

My great-grandfather was also a great Slavophile,
a folklorist.

KATHERINA

Sadness is the spiritual genius of the Slavic peoples.

BONFILA

Uh-huh.
   He wrote that the revolts of the Old Believers against
Peter the Great were early stirrings of the Revolution
among the peoples.

KATHERINA

Peter the Great, 1672-1725.

BONFILA

My great-grandfather also collected icons. And he
planned the Lenin Cult.

KATHERINA

Lenin: 1870-1923.

BONFILA

1924. When Lenin died, peasants from Tsarskoe Selo
sent this to my great-grandpa, to put in the tomb.

*(She unwraps the package. It's an old icon, with a metal
candleholder attached, in which is a red glass, inside of which
is a candle.)*

BONFILA

See? It's Lenin. They painted his face over an icon of St
Sergius of Radonezh, who lived six hundred years ago...

(Little pause. KATHERINA *drinks most of the rest of the
vodka, passes the last swallow to* BONFILA, *who drinks it.)*

BONFILA

...and who is said to have been a great worker of
miracles.

KATHERINA

We need more vodka.

BONFILA

There is no more vodka.

KATHERINA

We must go out and get some more vodka.

BONFILA

It's too late. It must be four a.m. There won't be a store
open.

KATHERINA

Why won't you make love to me?

BONFILA

Here?

KATHERINA

Oh, who gives a fuck where? Sure, here. If you love me
what would it matter.

BONFILA

Too creepy.

KATHERINA

Do it, here. Put your hand down my coveralls, slip it
deep inside me, blow hot fog-breath in my ears 'till my
brains cook, let me lick your cunt till my whole face is
wet, put my hair in your mouth, nip my buttocks, let
me scream joyfully as if a hungry animal I want to feed
is eating me up!

BONFILA

You embarrass me.

KATHERINA

You're afraid of sex with me.

BONFILA

Nonsense. *(Little pause)* I'm afraid of sex with you in
front of a Deputy Secretary of....

KATHERINA

He's off shooting himself.
   We're alone. I still have all my clothes on. Something's
wrong.

BONFILA

He won't shoot himself, and tomorrow he'll have us
both arrested. Ten years in an institution!

KATHERINA

Under Gorbachev people will not be...

BONFILA

(Overlap) Or maybe he'll have me transferred, just me, alone, to some godforsaken town in Uzbekistan; it was very, very, very stupid of you to kiss me like that in the open like that, to....

KATHERINA

He's probably dead by now—Poppy—and anyway he wouldn't...

BONFILA

(Overlap, continuous from above) ...to draw down attention like that, to deliberately....
HOW THE HELL DO YOU KNOW WHAT HE'D....
You're ignorant. You don't know anything.

(Pause)

KATHERINA

St Sergius of Radonezh. 1314-1392.
You're yelling because you're afraid of me.

BONFILA

Yes.

(They kiss. It gets hot, then hotter, then cold.)

BONFILA

Sexual deviance is symptomatic of cultures of luxury, in which monied classes cultivate morbid fascinations with biological functions, especially sex, tending towards narcissistic, antisocial, unproductive behavior such as...

Anyway, I don't believe in lesbians, I believe in the working class as the only repository for real historical

agency.
  You're right, I am afraid of you.

KATHERINA

Why did you come?

BONFILA

To show you this. *(The icon)*
  My great-grandmother is dying. She's one hundred
and five years old. Endurance is the spiritual genius of
Slavic peoples.
  She gave me this. She says it still works miracles.

KATHERINA

Who do you pray to when you light the candle, Lenin
or St Sergius?

BONFILA

She didn't say.

KATHERINA

What miracles has it worked?

BONFILA

She didn't say that either.

KATHERINA

Let's pray for vodka.

BONFILA

Shouldn't it be for something less frivolous?

KATHERINA

I pray for you to love me enough to be true to your
promise.

BONFILA

What promise?

KATHERINA
That you'll never leave me.

BONFILA
'Till you're sober.

KATHERINA
(Very serious) Then I must never be sober again.
Let's pray for vodka.

BONFILA
Match.

*(KATHERINA gives her one. BONFILA lights the candle.
The room darkens. KATHERINA kneels, bows her head.)*

KATHERINA
St Lenin or St Sergius, whoever you are. Please hear the
prayer of your little daughter. Look down on her from
heaven, she's in the room of dead brains; send vodka.
So that I may stay pathetically drunk so that she will
never leave me, because I'm full of violence and
self-pity and lies, but I do have decent feelings, too,
and dreams that are beautiful, that I'm not ashamed of
having, and there was no earthly thing I could attach
them to until I made her love me. Please help me little
father. Please hear my prayer.

(Pause)

(A BIG BABUSHKA enters, covered in snow.)

BIG BABUSHKA
(No pauses) Kat, I'll tell you what, I was sweeping the
snow off the steps up front and along comes this huge
truckload of soldiers plowing down the street, sliding
on the ice and bang it smacks into a telephone pole and
goes over on its side and all the soldiers come tumbling
out, and I rush over to see was anyone hurt, and
someone was because a soldier's running up and down

the street spattering blood in the snow and we can't get
him to stop because naturally they're all drunken idiots
from the sticks and he's screaming, "I'm dying, I'm
dying, Mother, Mother," and all the yelling frightens a
dog who bites a cop who swings a club which smashes
a big store window; dog, glass, blood, soldiers, and
finally we got the boy calmed down and sent him off
wrapped up in a bandage and the dogs run off and the
cop sees it's a liquor store window he's smashed so he
gives me a big bottle of this vodka to shut me up about
it (because everyone knows my mouth) which I can't
drink because my liver's already the size of my head
and so here, I've brought it to you, you drunken slut,
because I'm fond of you as if you were my own
granddaughter, now I got to go finish sweeping the
snow before more falls. (*The* BIG BABUSHKA *slams a big
bottle of vodka down on the table. She squints at the icon.*)
St Sergius of Radonezh with the face of Great Lenin.

(*She crosses herself and exits.*)

(KATHERINA *and* BONFILA *look at the vodka, and each other,
agape.*)

Scene Three

(*Even later.* KATHERINA *is asleep with her head in*
BONFILA*'s lap.* BONFILA *strokes* KATHERINA*'s hair and
looks at the icon, before which the candle is still burning.
The second bottle of vodka stands, almost empty, beside the
first empty bottle.*)

BONFILA
(*Very softly*) Little father: You left us alone and see the
state we've fallen into? Shouldn't you come back to us
now? We have suffered and suffered and Paradise has
not arrived. Shouldn't you come back and tell us what
went wrong?

She says your brain is in a jar next door. Your body
is across town. Pull yourself together, leave your tomb,
come claim your brain, remember speech, and action,
and once more, having surveyed the wreckage we have
made, tell your children: What is to be done?
  Shouldn't you come back now?

(Little red candle lights blink on everywhere.)

BONFILA
(Like on Christmas morning) Kat. Wake up. Kat. Wake
up. Katherina.

KATHERINA
What?

BONFILA
(Looking about at the lights, wonderingly) Do you...

KATHERINA
(Asleep) What is it?

BONFILA
(Standing) Do you see? Do you see? It's....

*(A little girl, dressed in a skirt and pullover sweater,
enters, and silently looks at* BONFILA. BONFILA *screams.*
KATHARINA *stands up abruptly.)*

KATHERINA
(Terrified, blind) I drank too much. Much too much.
I've blinded myself. *(She gropes about for* BONFILA*)* B! B!
Don't leave me! Don't leave me!
The lights are going out.

(The lights go out.)

ACT THREE

Scene One

(Talmenka, Siberia; 1992. A white room in a medical facility. The little girl who appeared at the end of Act Two, VODYA DOMIK, is now sitting in a wooden chair. She is expressionless, and mostly very still, although she blinks and occasionally, though infrequently, scratches her arm or shifts in the chair. She sits alone for a few beats. RODENT enters, wearing hat, coat, mittens, muffler, umbrella, galoshes. He's carrying a cheap, overstuffed briefcase. He is, as always, timorous and deferential, but in the intervening years he's gotten nasty. He tries to hide this; as the scene progresses, it emerges.)

(An old samovar stands in the corner, dead cold. Near it a kettle on a hotplate. RODENT looks at VODYA, who stares ahead. Several beats pass.)

RODENT

Hello little girl.

(VODYA has no reaction whatsoever, and has none throughout what follows. RODENT's tone is maddeningly unvaried: mild, cheerful, each attempt exactly the same as the one preceding, rather like a parrot.)

RODENT

Hello little girl.
Hello little girl.
Hello.

Hello.
Hello little girl.
Hello little girl.
Hello little girl.
Hello. Hello. Hello. Little girl.
(Pause. He thinks, then:)
Hello little girl.
Hello little girl.
Hello little girl. *(Getting a little ratty-panicky)*
Hello. Hello. Hello little girl. Little girl.
Little girl.
Little...

(He pauses again to look around and to think.)

*(*BONFILA *comes in, looking different—older, more tired—than in the previous act.* RODENT *doesn't hear her come in.)*

RODENT

Hello little girl.
Hello little girl.
Hello little girl.

BONFILA

She doesn't....

RODENT

(Badly frightened) OH!!

BONFILA

She doesn't speak. Deputy Councilor Rodent?

RODENT

(Shaken, nervous) Assistant Deputy Councilor.
Rodent, um, yes.
(Inclining his head towards VODYA*)* She...is...mute?
Deaf-mute, or...?

*(*BONFILA *shrugs.)*

BONFILA

Welcome to Talmenka.

(She exits. RODENT *looks at the door through which she has
exited, then turns back to* VODYA, *looks at her for a minute
and then, exactly as before:)*

RODENT

Hello little girl.
Hello little girl.
Hello little girl.
Hello little girl.
Want a boiled sweet?
(Mildly malicious) No, I don't have any boiled sweets.
Hello little girl.
Hello little girl.
Hello little...

*(*MRS SHASTLIVYI DOMIK, VODYA*'s mother, enters
abruptly. She is dressed pretty much like a young babushka.
She isn't loud but every word she speaks is a bullet aimed at
the person she's addressing.* RODENT *spins to face her.)*

MRS DOMIK

Her name is Vodya. Domik.

RODENT

Why doesn't she....

MRS DOMIK

She doesn't.

*(*MRS DOMIK *exits abruptly.* RODENT *looks at* VODYA.
A beat, then:)

RODENT

Hello little girl.
Hello little...

*(*BONFILA *and* MRS DOMIK *enter together.)*

BONFILA

Assistant Deputy Councilor Y T Rodent, this is Mrs Shastlivyi Domik, the child's mother.

MRS DOMIK

Her name is Vodya.

BONFILA

Assistant Deputy Councilor Rodent has come from Moscow. He's come to make a report to President Yeltsin.

RODENT

(Nervous little laugh, then:) Well, not directly to...

BONFILA

(Overlap) He's come to see what's going on here. About the children.

(They all look at VODYA.)

RODENT

(Official, but still nervous) Can she hear what we say?

BONFILA

Probably.

RODENT

But she doesn't speak.

BONFILA

No.

RODENT

Can she, I mean is she...

BONFILA

Theoretically, yes, I mean she's able, she has a larynx, a tongue, she.... So theoretically, yes, but...

MRS DOMIK
(Overlapping on second "theoretically") She doesn't speak.
She never speaks.

RODENT
How old is she?

BONFILA and MRS DOMIK
(Together) Eight.

(Pause)

RODENT
I...
(Nervous laugh)
Well how horrible.

(Pause)

BONFILA
Several of the children have died before their sixth
birthdays. She's the oldest. She's our survivor.

RODENT
I thought...um, I was told she'd be, um, um, um, yellow.

BONFILA
They're all yellow at birth, we have no idea why, really,
but. That's why they're called Yellow Children. The
jaundice fades by their first birthday.
The older they get the more we see it. Nervous-system
damage, renal malformation, liver, cataracts at three,
bone-marrow problems.

RODENT
See what?

BONFILA
What?

RODENT

You said, "The more we see it." What is "it"?

BONFILA

(A beat, then a bit more assertive, confrontational)
They mostly don't walk until.... How old was Vodya?

MRS DOMIK

Four.

BONFILA

And they don't speak. A few have words, minimal
speech, she doesn't.
   We've ruled out pretty much everything you'd
normally look for: pesticides, industrial pollutants,
something the parents are eating. They eat badly here
but...

MRS DOMIK

We've always eaten badly.

(Little pause)

RODENT

So it isn't the diet.

MRS DOMIK

We've always eaten badly.

BONFILA

It's genetic. Inherited. Probably chromosome alteration
due to her parents' exposure to ionizing radiation.
   Or her parents' parents. In significantly high doses,
wave, not particulate, not on the ground or on food,
but from a....
   In 1949, two hundred and fifty miles from here,
in Kazakhstan, in the Semipalatinsk area, the army
detonated a nuclear warhead. They detonated the

warhead to put out a minor oil fire. An experiment.
No one of course was evacuated.

RODENT

(Shrugs sadly) Stalin.

BONFILA

(Even more aggressive) The place I worked in last year,
Chelyabinsk, there's a cave, full of something in leaky
barrels. Unmarked railway cars used to pass through
the town late at night, smoking, on their way to the
cave, you could smell the fumes everywhere. Not
Stalin. Last year.

RODENT

It's a storage facility.

BONFILA

So, basically, you ask what's wrong with her. Well, in
my opinion and in the opinion of my colleagues, she's a
mutation. A nuclear mutant. Third generation. She has
a sister who's healthy; I wonder what her children will
be like?

RODENT

(To MRS DOMIK*)* I'm sorry.

*(*MRS DOMIK *walks out.)*

BONFILA

In Altograd, which is where I was before I was in
Chelyabinsk, there's twenty times the normal rate
for thyroid cancer. There's a lake full of blind fish.
Everyone has nosebleeds. Everyone's chronically
fatigued. Leukemia is epidemic. The reactor plant near
there has cracks in the casing, steam comes through
several times a month, it's the same kind as at
Chernobyl, it was supposed to be closed, it isn't, and
the caves in Chelyabinsk? The stuff you have in there,

probably cesium, strontium, certainly bomb-grade
plutonium, piled up since when? 1950? It's seeping into
the aquifer; sixty feet per year. Do you know what that
means? There's a river nearby. Millions drink from it.
This is documented. The Dnieper's already shot from
Chernobyl, and people still drink from that. Millions.
The plutonium in that cave. Three hundred pounds of
it could kill every person on the planet. You have thirty
tons down there, in rusting drums. The people of
Altograd voted for you to move it, a referendum,
last year: Why? Why hasn't it been moved?

RODENT

To where?

BONFILA

The whole country's a radioactive swamp, waste
dumps, warheads, malfunctioning reactors, there are
six hundred nuclear waste sites in Moscow, for God's
sake. Hundreds upon hundreds of thousands of people
have been exposed.

(Little pause)

RODENT

The world has changed with an unimaginable rapidity.
People grow impatient. Everything is new now, and
everything is terrible. In the old days I would not have
been forced to do this sort of work. *(With a little menace)*
In the old days you would not speak to me like this.

(Little pause)

BONFILA

All I ever see are the regional authorities, and they're
just the same old Party bosses who just....

RODENT

(Official) But you see, Doctor, there's nothing to be done.
We have no place to put it. We used to dump it into
the sea, the.... That's frowned on by the International
Community, its understandable, they'll take away our
loans if we.... We have no money. Trillions. It would
cost trillions. And some of these places will simply
never be inhabitable again. Regardless of the money.
Twenty thousand years.

(MRS DOMIK slams back into the room, stands glowering.)

RODENT

And anyway, we're broke.

BONFILA

And now you're offering to process and store
radioactive and toxic waste from the West.

RODENT

(Overlap) They'll pay us.

BONFILA

(Overlap) But store it where?

RODENT

(Overlap) We need the money. The Russian People need
the...

BONFILA

(Overlap) You've conducted tests. On uninformed
citizens. Whole populations, the Russian People...

RODENT

(Overlap, snide) I, personally, never did that.

BONFILA

(Overlap) The West doesn't do that. Expose its citizens
unknowingly to radiation, to.... Even the United States
would never do that.

RODENT

Oh don't be so certain...

BONFILA

I am...certain, the Western democracies, even capitalist
countries, don't....

RODENT

(Overlap) Then move to the West. Anyone can, now.
If they'll let you in. Which of course they won't.
What do you want from me?

BONFILA

I want to know.

RODENT

What?

BONFILA

BECAUSE I AM...STILL, A SOCIALIST! Isn't that
absurd! After all I've seen I still believe.... And, and I
want to know! And you, SOMEONE MUST TELL ME!
How this... How this came to pass. How any of this
came to pass. In a socialist country. In the world's first
socialist country.

(Little pause)

RODENT

Naiveté.

BONFILA

It's the spiritual genius of Slavic peoples.

RODENT
(A brief pause; trying to figure her out, now he's got the upper hand) What are you doing in Siberia.

BONFILA
I was transferred by the Ministry of Health Services in 1985.

RODENT
You must have made someone angry.

BONFILA
As a matter of fact I did. Not angry, jealous. He had me transferred.

RODENT
But things are different now. You could go back.

BONFILA
Yes.

RODENT
In fact, you could have gone back there five years ago, in 1987 you could have gone back. *(With mock enthusiasm)* Perestroika!

BONFILA
I suppose so. I was afraid.

RODENT
Of the man who had you transferred?

BONFILA
No.
Someone I disappointed. I disappointed a friend, I hurt her, badly, and I was afraid to face her again. So I stayed here.
Why are you asking me...?

RODENT

(Shrug, nasty smile) The Steppes, the Taiga, it's an
unhealthy place. Siberia, Doctor, is making you shrill.

MRS DOMIK

(Suddenly, to RODENT, *very upset)* Compensation.
Money. You're from Moscow, do you understand me?

RODENT

Yes, I understand what comp...

MRS DOMIK

*(Continuous from above, and throughout this section she
runs right over what* RODENT *says, taking only little breaths
when he begins to speak.)* I want to be compensated.
Look at her. Look. She'll never be anything.

RODENT

I'm truly sorry about your....

MRS DOMIK

(Overlap) I will need to be compensated. Look. Look.
What am I supposed to do with....

RODENT

I have forms for you to fill out and....

MRS DOMIK

(Overlap) How am I supposed to feed her? You cut back
on my assistance....

RODENT

It's very hard all over Russia, Mrs....

MRS DOMIK

(Overlap) I can't live without my assistance and you
took most of it, it's a pittance, how am I supposed to
feed her, she eats, and watch her, she has to be watched
every second and you closed down the day hospital,

you cut assistance so compensate me. And medicine,
now I have to pay for medicine, more than half the
money we have goes for....

RODENT
Austerity measures are necessary to.... Doctor, can you
get her to....

MRS DOMIK
(Overlap) ...for medicine, and how do I pay for that
medicine is expensive when I can't work because what
work is there that pays, that really pays, and with
inflation....

RODENT
The transition to a free-market economy requires
sacrifice.

MRS DOMIK
(Overlap) ...my God, inflation, money's worthless
and who has what you need for the black market,
it's impossible, I should be compensated and....

RODENT
The World Bank is promising....

BONFILA
(Simultaneous with RODENT*)* Mrs Domik, I think you
should maybe sit and I'll get some tea...

MRS DOMIK
(Overlap)... and anyway who'll mind her if I work.
(To BONFILA*)* I DON'T WANT TEA, and what have you
ever done for her, huh, except tests and tests and tests,
you haven't helped any of the children, and she's not
dying she's growing, and who's supposed to mind her
if I have to work all day, she doesn't just sit now, she
wanders, across roads, and.... Well? WHAT ABOUT

MY DAUGHTER? WHAT ABOUT MY DAUGHTER?
WHAT ARE YOU GOING TO DO ABOUT MY
DAUGHTER? WHO'LL PAY FOR THAT?

BONFILA

Please, Mrs Domik, there are other patients in the....

MRS DOMIK

Take her!

(MRS DOMIK *yanks* VODYA *out of the chair and drags her
over to* RODENT, *who recoils with fear.* MRS DOMIK *shoves
the child against* RODENT.)

MRS DOMIK

She's not a, a, a person! NO! Take her to Yeltsin! Take
her to Gorbachev! Take her to Gaidar! Take her to
Clinton! YOU care for her! YOU did this! YOU did this!
She's YOURS.

(MRS DOMIK *exits.*)

(BONFILA *takes* VODYA *and leads her back to her chair.*)

RODENT

Um, um, um...

(BONFILA *goes out of the room.*)

(RODENT *goes over to* VODYA *and pats her on the head.*)

(MRS DOMIK *comes back in, alone, wearing a coat and scarf,
and carrying the same for* VODYA.)

MRS DOMIK

Get your filthy fucking hands off my child.

(RODENT *moves away from* VODYA, *sits.* MRS DOMIK
bundles VODYA *up, preparing to leave.*)

RODENT

(Quietly, carefully, furtively) Mrs Domik, may I speak to
you, not as a representative of the government but in
confidence, as one Russian to another?
(Little pause) This nation is falling apart. It is in the
hands of miscreants and fools. The government does
not serve the people, but betrays the people to foreign
interests. The tragedy of your daughter is but one
instance, a tragic instance of the continuance of the
crimes of the Communist era through to the present
day. Chaos threatens. The land is poisoned. The United
States is becoming our landlord. Dark-skinned people
from the Caucasus regions, Muslims, Asiatics, swarthy
inferior races have flooded Moscow, and white
Christian Russians such as you and I are expected
to support them. There is no order and no strength;
the army is bound hand and foot by foreign agents
pretending to be our leaders, but they are not our
leaders. They stand idly by as the United Nations
imposes sanctions and threatens war against our
brother Slavs in Serbia who are fighting to liberate
Bosnia; the great Pan-Slavic Empire has been stolen
from us again by the International Jew. Not because we
are weak; we have enormous bombs, chemicals, secret
weapons. Because we lack a leader, a man of iron and
will; but the leader is coming, Mrs Domik, already he is
here, already I and millions like us who have joined the
Liberal Democratic Party of Russia support him. We
need more women. Motherland, Mrs Domik, is the
spiritual genius of Slavic peoples. *(Reaching in his
briefcase)* Would you like some literature?

(He proffers a pamphlet; MRS DOMIK *takes it, looks it over as
if examining a rotten piece of fruit. She fixes* RODENT *with a
look, smiling in an ugly way, then crumples his pamphlet
and drops it on the floor.)*

MRS DOMIK

(Smiling) Listen, you fucking ferret, I'm not a fucking "Russian like you," I'm a Lithuanian, and I fucking hate Russians; and why am I here in Siberia, because fucking Stalin sent my grandma here fifty years ago. My grandpa and my great-uncles and great-aunts died tunneling through the Urals on chain gangs. Their father and his brother were shot in Vilnius, their children were shot fighting Germans, my sister starved to death, and my brother killed himself under fucking Brezhnev after fifteen years in a psychiatric hospital, I've tried twice to do the same—and my daughter....

Fuck this century. Fuck your leader. Fuck the state. Fuck all governments, fuck the motherland, fuck your mother, your father, and you.

(MRS DOMIK *takes* VODYA's *hand and exits.*)

(RODENT, *ashen with terror, puts his literature back in his briefcase, stands, begins to put his coat and gear on.*)

(BONFILA *enters.*)

BONFILA

Leaving?

RODENT

Mm-hmm.

BONFILA

Would you like to meet more of the children?

RODENT

Er, um, no, no, not necessary.

BONFILA

We could go through files....

RODENT

Send them to my office, send them to Moscow.
(Little pause)

BONFILA

I also didn't go back to Moscow.... You know when you
asked me earlier? Why didn't I go back? Because I
thought I could do some good here. In the face of all
this impossibility, twenty thousand years, that little girl
who won't live five more years, I still believe that good
can be done, that there's work to be done. Good hard
work.

RODENT

(A little smile) To the Motherland. To the work ahead.
Goodbye.

(He exits.)

*(*BONFILA *is alone for a beat. She kicks the little chair in
which* VODYA *had been sitting, sending it clattering across
the room.)*

(Another brief beat, and then KATHERINA *enters, dressed in
a medical assistant's coat.)*

KATHERINA

I'm dying for a smoke. Did you remember the
cigarettes?

*(*BONFILA *takes a pack of cigarettes out of her labcoat pocket,
and gives them to* KATHERINA.*)*

BONFILA

They're bad for your health.

KATHARINA

Yeah, yeah. To Moscow. I want to go to Moscow.

BONFILA

You say that every single day.

KATHARINA

Some day you'll say yes.

BONFILA

Are you sorry you followed me here?

KATHARINA

I didn't follow you, you begged me to come.
Siberia sucks.
I'm done for the day. Are you ready for home?

BONFILA

I'm ready.

EPILOGUE

(UPGOBKIN and PRELAPSARIANOV are in Heaven, a gloomy, derelict place resembling a city after an earthquake. They are dressed in high fur hats and greatcoats. Snow falls on them. They are seated on wooden crates. Between them is another crate they are using as a table. They are playing cards.
A samovar stands on a fourth crate, brewing tea.)

UPGOBKIN

I spent my many years on Earth loud in proclaiming the faith that there is no God.

PRELAPSARIANOV

Now you have been dead almost ten years. What do you think now?

UPGOBKIN

I am bewildered. I expected more from the Afterlife, in the way of conclusive proof, in some form or another....

PRELAPSARIANOV

But the Ancient of Days remains evasive, ineffable, in Heaven as on Earth.

Heaven, I had been led to believe in my childhood, was not such a dark and gloomy place, which forces upon me the suspicion that my mother lied to me each night as I knelt by my bed, praying; a suspicion I cannot entertain.

Your deal.

UPGOBKIN

And I must admit I am tired of playing cards with you, Aleksii Antedilluvianovich.

PRELAPSARIANOV

I believe I have improved my card game considerably, Serge Esmereldovich.

UPGOBKIN

After ten years of playing, Aleksii, it would actually be more interesting to me if your game had not improved.
    Can we think of nothing else to do?

PRELAPSARIANOV

We could look down on the Earth, see how things are going for Russia.

(Little pause)

UPGOBKIN

Let's not.

PRELAPSARIANOV

The Party seems to have become popular again....

UPGOBKIN

As I was saying, let's not look.

PRELAPSARIANOV

Your deal.

UPGOBKIN

Tea?

(PRELAPSARIANOV *nods "yes"*; UPGOBKIN *gets the tea.*)

PRELAPSARIANOV

We could look down on the Earth and see how things are going elsewhere. Cuba. Rwanda. Bosnia. Pakistan. *(Beat)* Afghanistan?

UPGOBKIN

God forbid.

PRELAPSARIANOV

Yes, perhaps not. It is depressing.

UPGOBKIN

It is very depressing.

PRELAPSARIANOV

It is.

UPGOBKIN

(Getting very frustrated) I had at least expected to see, if not the face of God or the face of Absolute Nothingness, then the Future, at least the Future: But ahead there is only a great cloud of turbulent midnight, and not even the dead can see what is to come.

(VODYA DOMIK *enters.)*

PRELAPSARIANOV

(Moved, sad, wondering) Look, Serge, a child has come.

UPGOBKIN

Hello little girl.

VODYA

Hello.

PRELAPSARIANOV

How sad to see a little one wandering Night's Plutonian Shore.

VODYA

Plutonium? Is there plutonium even here?

PRELAPSARIANOV

No, no, Plutonian-n-n-n, not plutonium-m-m-m. I was
quoting the great American poet, Edgar Allan Poe.

UPGOBKIN

I prefer Emerson. So dialectical! But moral and spiritual
too, like Dostoevsky. If Dostoevsky had lived in
America, and had had a sunnier disposition, he might
have been Emerson. They were contemporaries. The
world is fantastical! I miss it so.

PRELAPSARIANOV

(To VODYA) Welcome to Nevermore.

UPGOBKIN

How did you die, child?

VODYA

Cancer, a wild profusion of cells; dark flowerings in my
lungs, my brain, my blood, my bones; dandelion and
morning glory vine seized and overwhelmed the field;
life in my body ran riot. And here I am.

PRELAPSARIANOV

I died from speaking too much.

UPGOBKIN

I died from leaping.

PRELAPSARIANOV

He leapt, he died, and still he cannot see the New.

UPGOBKIN

It is bitter.

VODYA

The socialist experiment in the Soviet Union has failed,
Grandfathers.

PRELAPSARIANOV

It has.

VODYA

And what sense are we to make of the wreckage?
Perhaps the principles were always wrong. Perhaps
it is true that social justice, economic justice, equality,
community, an end to master and slave, the withering
away of the state: These are desirable but not realizable
on the Earth. *(Little pause)*

Perhaps the failure of socialism in the East speaks
only of the inadequacy and criminal folly of any
attempt to organize more equitably and rationally the
production and distribution of the wealth of nations.
And chaos, market fluctuations, rich and poor,
colonialism and war are all that we shall ever see.
(Little pause)

Perhaps, even, the wreckage that became the Union of
Soviet Socialist Republics is so dreadful to contemplate
that the histories and legends of Red October, indeed of
hundreds of years of communitarian, millenarian, and
socialist struggle, will come to seem mere prelude to
Stalin, the gulags, the death of free thought, dignity,
and human decency; and "socialist" become a foul
epithet; and to the ravages of Capital there will be no
conceivable alternative.

PRELAPSARIANOV

It is bitter.

UPGOBKIN

It is very bitter.

VODYA

I am inexpressibly sad, Grandfathers. Tell me a story.

(Little pause)

UPGOBKIN

I have this one story, a Russian story....

PRELAPSARIANOV

Whatever they do, whatever the glory or ignominy, as we move through history, Russians make great stories.

UPGOBKIN

I have this one story, but I can say only that it happened, and not what it means.

(VODYA *climbs up on his lap.*)

UPGOBKIN

Vladimir Ilyich Ulyanov was very sad. He was seventeen years old, and the secret police had just hanged his brother, Sasha, for having plotted to kill the Czar. All this was long ago. Because he already missed his brother very much, Vladimir, who was to become Great Lenin, decided to read his brother's favorite book: a novel, by Chernyshevsky, the title and contents of which asked the immortal question; which Lenin asked and in asking stood the world on its head; the question which challenges us to both contemplation and, if we love the world, to action; the question which implies: Something is terribly wrong with the world, and avers: Human beings can change it; the question asked by the living and, apparently, by the fretful dead as well: What is to be done?

(*Little pause*)

VODYA

What is to be done?

PRELAPSARIANOV

Yes. What is to be done?

END